Cambridge English Readers

....

Level 3

Series editor: Philip Prowse

No Place to Hide

Alan Battersby

D1105084

CAMBRIDGE UNIVERSITY PRESS
Cambridge, New York, Melbourne, Madrid, Cape Town, Singapore,
São Paulo, Delhi, Dubai, Tokyo, Mexico City

Cambridge University Press
The Edinburgh Building, Cambridge CB2 8RU, UK

www.cambridge.org
Information on this title: www.cambridge.org/9780521169752

© Cambridge University Press 2011

This publication is in copyright. Subject to statutory exception
and to the provisions of relevant collective licensing agreements,
no reproduction of any part may take place without the written
permission of Cambridge University Press.

First published 2011

Printed in China by Sheck Wah Tong Printing Press Limited

A catalogue record of this publication is available from the British Library

ISBN 978-0-521-16975-2 Paperback
ISBN 978-0-521-17305-6 Paperback with audio CDs (2) Pack

Cambridge University Press has no responsibility for the persistence or
accuracy of URLs for external or third-party internet websites referred to in
this publication, and does not guarantee that any content on such websites is,
or will remain, accurate or appropriate.

Alan Battersby has asserted his right to be identified as the Author of the Work in
accordance with the Copyright, Designs and Patents Act 1988.

No character in this work is based on any person living or dead.
Any resemblance to an actual person or situation is purely accidental.

Map artwork by Malcolm Barnes
Cover image: Thinkstock

Contents

Characters

Nat Marley: a New York private investigator
Stella Delgado: Nat Marley's personal assistant
Patrick O'Neill: an accountant at Ocean Star Finance
Joyce O'Neill: Patrick O'Neill's wife
Julia O'Neill: Patrick and Joyce O'Neill's daughter
Ronald Steinmann: Patrick O'Neill's head of department
Lorraine Houston: the president of Ocean Star Finance
Ed Winchester: a reporter on the *Daily News*
Brett Johnson: a financial reporter on the *Daily News*
Captain Oldenberg: a detective with the New York Police Department (NYPD)
Joe Blaney: a colleague of Nat Marley, ex-NYPD
Frank Van Zandt: the owner of Frankie's Cocktail Lounge
Gina: a receptionist at the Metro Hotel

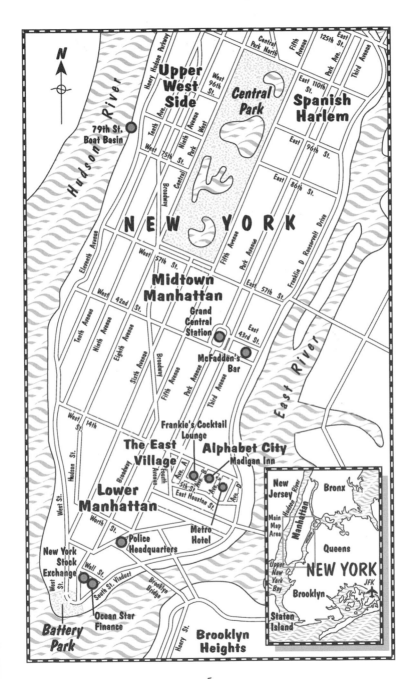

N

Hudson River

79th St.
Boat Basin

Henry Hudson Parkway

Upper
West
Side

West 96th St.

Central
Park

Central Park North

Fifth Avenue

East 125th St.

Park Ave.

Third Avenue

East 110th St.

Spanish
Harlem

East 96th St.

East 86th St.

Tenth Ave.

Ninth Avenue

Park Avenue

West 75th St.

Broadway

Central Park

N E W   Y O R K

Eleventh Avenue

West 57th St.

Fifth Avenue

Park Avenue

Franklin D Roosevelt Drive

West 42nd St.

Midtown
Manhattan

East 57th St.

Tenth Avenue

Ninth Avenue

Eighth Avenue

Broadway

Grand
Central
Station

East 43rd St.

McFadden's
Bar

East River

Sixth Avenue

Fifth Avenue

Park Avenue

Third Avenue

West 14th

West St.

Frankie's Cocktail
Lounge

The East
Village

Alphabet City

Madigan Inn

Hudson St.

Broadway

Fourth Avenue

Ave. A

Ave. B

Ave. C

Ave. D

5th St.

Lower
Manhattan

East Houston St.

West St.

Worth St.

Police
Headquarters

Metro
Hotel

New York
Stock
Exchange

Wall St.

South St. Viaduct

Brooklyn
Bridge

West St.

Ocean Star
Finance

Battery
Park

Henry St.

Brooklyn
Heights

New
Jersey

Hudson River

Bronx

Main
Map
Area

Manhattan

Queens

Upper
New
York
Bay

NEW YORK

JFK

Brooklyn

Staten
Island

Chapter 1   *New York City in fall*

Monday, October 4th. A cool, clear morning with the promise of a fine day ahead. Fall is my favorite season in this city – the break between summer heat and winter cold. It's a time when you're not trying to escape the worst of New York's weather. In the city parks, leaves on the trees were just beginning to turn red and gold.

The name's Nat Marley, licensed private investigator. Before I became an investigator, I used to be a police officer – a cop with the NYPD, the New York Police Department. Since then, I've worked for myself. So what does "private investigator" make you think of? A cool handsome guy with an exciting, sometimes dangerous, job? Think again. Some of the time I'm looking for missing persons. Or maybe I'm watching a husband to find out if he's seeing another woman. And when I look in the mirror, I see an ordinary guy in his forties who's losing his hair.

As usual, I caught the number seven subway train from my home in Flushing Main Street, Queens, to Midtown Manhattan.

Through Queens, the subway runs above the streets. Below you can see different areas, each home to people from around the world – Flushing: Chinese and Koreans, Corona Heights: Central and South Americans. At Grand Central Station I picked up two coffees. Crowds of New Yorkers were hurrying out onto 42nd Street. Then, like any other day, I walked the couple of blocks to my office at 220, East 43rd Street.

My personal assistant, Stella Delgado, was already at her desk opening the mail. She's a smart, good-looking Puerto Rican who understands everything about computers. She's been with me for most of the time I've been a private investigator. Stella comes from Spanish Harlem, on the Upper East Side of Manhattan – a part of the city where tourists don't go. On the streets there you'll hear more Spanish than English. She never finished school, but later, as an adult, went to night school. She's worked hard for what she has now – a job, comfortable home and loving family.

"How are you doing, Stella?" I asked. "I got coffee for you."

"Thanks. I'm fine," she replied. "Could you leave it on the desk?"

A knock at the door. Two women entered. One, a lady in her middle fifties, dressed in a dark green suit. The suit looked expensive, but she looked worried. The other, a young woman in her twenties. I compared their faces – they had to be mother and daughter.

"Do I have the right place?" said the mother. "This is the Marley Detective Agency?"

"That's correct, ma'am. The name's Nat Marley. What can I do for you?" I asked.

"Well, it's kind of difficult ..." she started.

"Come through to my office and take a seat," I said. "Your names, please?"

"I'm Joyce O'Neill and this is my daughter, Julia," said the mother. "It's about my husband, Patrick. He's disappeared and I really need to find him. It doesn't matter how much it costs."

"I'm very sorry to hear that, ma'am," I said. "Let's take it slowly, from the beginning."

She looked at me with large sad eyes. "I haven't seen him since Saturday night. When I woke up Sunday morning, he was gone. He left this message on the kitchen table." She took a postcard from her purse and read to me:

"My dear Joyce. Don't worry. I'm safe, but I can't come home. The thing is, I know something which puts me and maybe you in danger. Don't phone me, or my office or the NYPD. If anyone asks for me, say I'm out of town. Trust me. Stay at Julia's place and wait for my call. All my love. Patrick."

"I have an apartment in Hamilton Heights, near Columbia University," Julia explained. "Mom has been staying with me there since Sunday."

"Mr. Marley, I'm worried sick," Joyce O'Neill continued. "Patrick's never done anything like this before."

I knew it could be bad news when someone disappears. But I didn't want to make her any more worried than she was already.

"There can be many reasons why someone disappears," I said. "Let's not expect the worst. Did your husband call?"

She nodded. "He's OK, but said he had to hide while he decided what to do. He wouldn't tell me what was happening. He just said the less I knew, the safer I would be. I just don't know what to do."

"It sounds like he's in immediate danger," I said. "It would be useful to know as much as possible about your husband."

I learned that Patrick O'Neill worked as an accountant. His employer was a firm on Wall Street called Ocean Star Finance. He had worked there for over ten years. His home address was Henry Street, Brooklyn Heights. His photograph showed a tall, gray-haired guy with black metal glasses, but there was nothing special about him. He had been married for twenty-three years. He was just an ordinary family man, with a daughter studying for her MBA at Columbia University.

"There must be a good reason why your husband asked you not to call his office. So tell me some more about his work," I said.

"Patrick's the second highest person in his department," Joyce O'Neill answered. "The head of department is Ronald Steinmann."

"What kind of guy is this Steinmann?" I asked.

"He's good at his job – excellent in fact, though he's not well liked. Patrick and Steinmann aren't the best of friends."

"A few more questions, if you don't mind," I continued. "Has your husband been acting strangely or differently in any way?"

She thought carefully before answering. "I can't say he has. His work's really important to him. He often has to work late, and he sometimes brings work home – that's normal."

"I'm afraid I have to ask this. Could there be another woman?" I asked her.

She looked at me angrily, then said, "Sorry. I guess it's your job to ask. My husband has never even looked at another woman."

"One final question," I said. "It's useful to know how carefully a missing person has planned to disappear. Has your husband taken anything with him? Did he pack clothes? Did he take the car?"

"The car's gone, and he took a travel bag with a change of clothes and some books," she replied.

"Thanks, ma'am. You've been really helpful," I said. "I'll do everything possible to find out what's happened. I'll need to visit you at your home later to look at your husband's papers and computer. That might give me some ideas. Could you meet me there at three o'clock?"

After Mrs O'Neill and her daughter had left, I looked out of the window. The sun was trying to make the gray buildings of East 43rd Street look beautiful. It would need to try harder. So a normal, hard-working guy had suddenly disappeared. He could be in serious trouble. I had thought this was going to be another ordinary day. My mistake.

Chapter 2 *Wall Street*

I told Stella what I'd learned so far. As I talked, her fingers flew over the computer keyboard.

"Take a look, Nat," she said. "The latest information from the Ocean Star Finance website."

It was an investment firm on Wall Street, the financial center of America. "Investment" meant lending out its clients' money on international money markets to make more money. So their already rich clients became even richer. Also, it seemed to be one of the best firms – a favorite of many famous New Yorkers. Year after year Ocean Star had returned excellent money to its clients. It was like a money-making machine.

The head of the firm was Lorraine Houston. She was well known to the public through TV talk shows and magazine stories about her homes on Long Island and in New England. Her clothes only came from the best stores. She'd lived the American Dream – the daughter of a poor New Jersey family who had become the president of Ocean Star.

I decided to call O'Neill's office and spoke with his personal assistant. I let her think I had some money to invest. Of course, it wasn't the truth – I've never had enough money to save much. But after fifteen years in the NYPD, I'd learned how to tell a good lie.

"This is Mr. Marley," I told her. "I'd like to meet with Mr. O'Neill this afternoon. I just wanted to check if he could see me at three thirty."

"I'm sorry," said the personal assistant. "Mr. O'Neill called this morning to say he was sick."

"Really? In that case, I'll have to speak to the head of department," I said.

"I'm afraid that's not possible," she replied. "You see, Mr. Steinmann doesn't work here anymore. He left the firm on Friday."

"Left the firm?" I asked. "Why? Did he find another job?"

"I couldn't say, sir," replied the personal assistant.

"Whose decision was this?" I asked.

"I don't know," she said.

"Do you mean you don't know or you're not allowed to tell me?" I asked.

"As I said before, sir, I really couldn't say," she said.

Something felt wrong. Both the head guys in the department had gone? Working at Ocean Star didn't seem too good for your health. Was it Steinmann's decision to leave? You know what they say when someone suddenly leaves a job? "Did he jump or was he pushed?"

Stella was going through the mail. I picked up the phone bill.

"Ouch! That's going to hurt my wallet!" I said. "Did we really make that many calls? Well, we'd better find Patrick O'Neill quickly and make ourselves some money. Come on, Stella. We're going to visit Wall Street. Let's see if we can find out anything more on Ocean Star."

Some investigators take cabs everywhere. Not me. If possible, I take public transportation, the New York subway. It's cheap, fast and much safer than it used to be when I was a cop. We took a train from Grand Central Station to Wall Street. While traveling downtown, I described a plan to

Stella. It was, of course, going to mean telling some more lies.

"When we get to Ocean Star, we check in with reception and let them think we're millionaires with money to invest. We'll tell them we need financial advice and ask to meet with one of their advisors immediately. Let's see what they can offer us. We'll act all unsure, and ask for promises that our investment will be completely safe. I'll do most of the talking and you watch the advisor."

From the subway station, we walked east, past the New York Stock Exchange. Outside the building, tourists were busy taking pictures. Ahead of us we could see the full height of the New Century Building. Thirty floors of glass and metal, a wall of silver in the sunshine. Ocean Star Finance used the top four floors.

At the reception desk, you could almost smell money in the air. The black office furniture looked expensive and the carpets were deep and soft. A meeting was soon organized. Yes, they wanted to talk to the millionaires. It's true what people say – money does open doors. The advisor gave complete answers to my questions and seemed to be sure of herself. Finally I asked, "So you can promise us a return of up to fifteen per cent on our investment by this time next year? No problem?"

"None at all," she said immediately. "You don't need to worry. We offer the best service on Wall Street."

Afterwards, I asked Stella for her thoughts. "You know, Nat, it was like listening to an actor who'd learned her lines well," she said. "She was giving the usual message: 'Don't worry. What could possibly go wrong?' But you know and I know that's not always the case in the world of finance."

I told Stella I was going to take an early lunch at McFadden's Bar to talk with the people from the *Daily News*.

The information I needed to know about Ocean Star couldn't be found on the internet. I wanted the inside information. McFadden's, on the corner of East 42nd Street and Second Avenue, was the second home of *Daily News* reporters. These guys often knew much more than they could write about in their newspaper – the kind of news that could be dangerous.

Inside the bar, the lunchtime crowd was beginning to come in. I looked around and saw a tall man with white hair among a group of younger reporters. He was Ed Winchester, a reporter who had been with the *Daily News* longer than I could remember. He had helped me several times in the past.

"Nat! Over here. And while you're at the bar, get me another drink," he called, waving an empty glass.

I knew that the price of information from Ed would be a beer, but that was cheap enough. I ordered two beers and went over to Ed. He had moved to an empty table and pushed a chair toward me.

"Well, Nat, what brings you here?" he asked. "You got that 'I need to know something' look on your face."

I described what had happened during the morning and what I already knew. "It seems kind of strange to me. One of the two head guys in the department has suddenly left and the other has disappeared on sick leave."

Ed thought carefully. "Finance isn't my field, but there's a young friend of mine who might be able to help." He went over to the reporters and returned with a guy in his twenties. "Nat, I'd like to introduce Brett Johnson, a financial reporter on the Wall Street page. Brett, Mr. Marley needs anything you might have on Ocean Star Finance."

"OK, Mr. Marley," Brett began. "There are two sides to the story. Each year, Ocean Star makes excellent money for its clients. How can they do it? Is it just luck? Or is Lorraine Houston really a financial superwoman?

"Second, if Ocean Star can make such good money, then why aren't all the other firms on Wall Street doing the same thing? However, I don't have all of the facts, so that's why you haven't read about it."

"Thanks, Brett. You've given me something to think about," I said.

Chapter 3 *Brooklyn Heights*

After lunch I met Stella at Grand Central Station by the information desk, under the big clock. We were going to see Joyce O'Neill at her home on Henry Street, Brooklyn Heights. As usual, we took the subway.

Henry Street is just one block away from the subway station. On either side of Henry Street are lines of old brownstone houses, built in the nineteenth century. We walked in the sunshine to the house.

The O'Neills opened the door before I could knock. Joyce O'Neill looked terrible – she was crying and her eyes were red. Julia was holding her mother's hand. "Please come in," said Mrs. O'Neill.

As she was speaking, the phone rang. She picked it up and said, "Joyce O'Neill speaking." Then she slowly put it down.

"Nobody there. That's the third time today," she told me.

"I'll check that number if I may?" I asked. I called the service to find out who last phoned. As I expected, it refused to give me a number. I didn't want to make Mrs. O'Neill any more worried. "No luck. It wouldn't tell me anything – maybe just a wrong number. But if it happens again, tell me. Now, this morning I called your husband's office at Ocean Star – I let them think I was a client. I was told he was on sick leave. And another thing. Steinmann has left the firm. I couldn't find out why."

"Really?" said Mrs. O'Neill. "What on earth's going on?"

"I wish I knew," I said. "While we're here, we'd like to find out more about your husband – his interests, what kind of person he is. You never know, any little thing could be important. Does he have a home office?"

"Sure, it's through here," said Mrs. O'Neill.

The room looked out onto the street. On either side of the window were pictures of old New York. Under the window was a desk with nine drawers and on the desk sat a computer. On the other walls were bookshelves.

"Ms. Delgado will look through your husband's computer files, if that's OK with you," I told her.

Stella turned on the computer, but of course, we needed the password.

Julia spelled it for Stella: "It's J-U-L-I-E. That's what my father always calls me."

While Stella continued with the computer, I began my search through the books. They were of little interest to us. Then I continued with the drawers of the desk. Again, I discovered nothing that might help us until I tried to open the final drawer – it was locked. But a minute's work with a small knife was enough to open it. It was full of books about card games, mainly poker. I read the titles: *Ninety-nine Ways to Win at Poker*, *Poker – Use Your Intelligence and Win*, *The Complete Poker Player* and so on.

O'Neill had read every book carefully. On most pages there were notes in pencil – the sort of notes that only a serious student of the game would make. Was he hiding the books from his wife? I showed them to Mrs. O'Neill.

"Could you tell me if this is your husband's handwriting?" I asked.

"Yes, that's Patrick's," she replied.

"Did you realize that your husband was interested in card games?" I asked her.

"I had no idea. It's a complete surprise. That's something he never talked about. And I thought I knew everything about him," she said sadly.

Stella opened O'Neill's email and I waited patiently as she checked through all the information. Finally, she was ready.

"Most of what I've opened here seems to be quite normal," said Stella. "Work letters mainly. But there's something here – the last email to Steinmann, sent on Friday afternoon. It reads, 'I didn't think you could be so stupid. I can't believe what you've done.'"

"Do you have any idea what this could be about?" I asked Mrs. O'Neill.

"It could be some kind of disagreement," she replied.

Stella needed Mrs. O'Neill's help to get into the family bank accounts. She entered the numbers and soon the information came up on the screen. There was a joint account in the names of Patrick and Joyce O'Neill, and also an account in Joyce O'Neill's name. The joint account seemed normal, as did Mrs. O'Neill's account. But we needed another password to open Patrick O'Neill's account.

Mrs. O'Neill went straight to the kitchen and returned with a little notebook. "Patrick said I should keep this in a safe place. If anything happened to him, I'd be able to find the information on the computer." She passed the book to Stella, who searched through it to find the necessary numbers. New information came on the screen and Stella now looked more serious.

"Mrs. O'Neill, do you know someone called F. Van Zandt?" she asked.

"I've never heard the name," she answered. "Why?"

"Well, if you look here, there have been several large payments to this Van Zandt over the last six months," Stella explained.

Mrs. O'Neill looked at the screen and put her hand to her mouth. "I just don't understand," she said. "This last payment is $15,000! And look here. Patrick took out $10,000 this morning."

"There's more," said Stella. "Two large payments to Steinmann during the past three months. Over $25,000."

"I really can't understand it," said Mrs. O'Neill.

"There must be a good reason," I said. "Van Zandt's an unusual name, so I hope it won't be too much trouble to find him – or her."

I had a good idea what was going on. O'Neill could be a secret poker player. Those payments could mean that he'd lost heavily at poker and was paying back the winner month by month. But why had he paid all that money to Steinmann?

Chapter 4 *A voice from the past*

Tuesday, October 5th. Stella and I were at East 43rd Street early. Now we had another person to find.

"Stella, see if you can find a phone number for this Van Zandt," I asked. "I'll look for a number for Steinmann."

My search was much faster than Stella's. It was all there in the phone book – the number and an address on West 75th Street, on the Upper West Side near Central Park. You needed serious money to live in that part of town.

I made the call. "Good morning. May I speak with Mr. Steinmann?" I asked.

"Who are you and what's your business with Mr. Steinmann?" answered a loud voice. A voice I knew very well – Captain Oldenberg of the NYPD. What was he doing there? I wondered.

"Oldenberg! Great to hear your voice again!" I said. "Remember me? Nat Marley. Why, it only seems like yesterday when we used to be cops together."

Oldenberg didn't want to talk about old times. "Just answer the question, Marley!" he shouted.

"OK, OK. I'm making the call for a client. Mr. Steinmann is the head of her husband's department. It's important that I speak with him."

"Very interesting," replied Oldenberg. "That's going to be kind of difficult. You see, Steinmann has disappeared. Nobody's seen him since Friday. How about you tell me what's going on?"

I knew I might need Oldenberg's help. I told myself to be patient. "My client's husband is in some kind of trouble," I said. "I thought his boss could help with a few questions."

"I get the picture," said Oldenberg. "As usual, you can't tell me the full story. But let me tell you this, Marley. Don't try hiding information that could help my investigation, or else I'll have you at Police Headquarters for questioning."

Message received and understood. Oldenberg was a good cop and was doing his job. But, as I knew from the old days with the NYPD, he was neither the friendliest nor the easiest guy to work with.

As soon as I put the phone down, it rang. It was Mrs. O'Neill. She had returned home to Henry Street to pick up a change of clothes and she had found the front door wide open. Someone had broken into the house. I remembered the calls that Mrs. O'Neill had received yesterday. Now I knew that someone was checking to see when the house was empty.

"Is anything missing?" I asked.

"I really don't know. Please come quickly. I'm so afraid they'll come back," she said.

"Don't touch anything," I told her. "Can you wait with a neighbor? … Good. I'm on my way."

I left Stella looking for phone numbers for Van Zandts. I took another subway ride to Brooklyn Heights. With the number of traffic lights between Midtown Manhattan and Brooklyn, the subway was always faster. I called Mrs. O'Neill's cellphone five minutes before I arrived. She was standing by the front door, her hands shaking.

"Mr. Marley, this is just horrible. It must be something to do with my poor Patrick," she cried.

She led me into the house. Someone had made a complete mess of the home office. All the books were off the shelves, with their pages open. Empty desk drawers were lying on the carpet. The computer was still there, but when I felt around the back of the machine, it was open. The hard drive was missing.

"Look here," I said. "That's what they were looking for – information on the hard drive. But if they don't find what they're looking for on the hard drive they could return and you'll be in serious danger. So I don't want you to return to this house again."

"I'll stay at Julia's until this is over," Mrs O'Neill said sadly.

"OK. We have to make sure this house is safe before you leave," I said. "I'll call a twenty-four hour lock service. You'll need new, stronger locks. I'll stay here while we wait."

I would probably have a couple of hours to wait with Mrs. O'Neill. It was a chance to ask a few more questions and get a better picture of her husband. I didn't think she realized how much danger she could be in. When would she agree to call the NYPD?

"Mrs. O'Neill, what can you tell me about your husband's boss, Steinmann?" I started. "Yesterday you said they weren't the best of friends."

"A couple of years ago, Patrick had the chance to become the department head. He was the right person for the job and he was well liked. Unfortunately, he didn't get the job, though that wasn't his fault. Lorraine Houston, the president, wanted someone fresh and new from outside. She preferred the kind of guy who didn't care if he wasn't liked. So Steinmann got the job. Patrick continued with his work as best as he could, but there was no friendship between him and Steinmann."

"Thanks. That's useful to know. Has your husband always lived in Brooklyn?" I went on.

"No. We moved here when Julia was just a kid. Patrick's family are Irish-American. His grandparents arrived in the U.S. from Dublin in the 1920s. They more or less got off the ship and moved straight to the East Village. Patrick grew up in Alphabet City, on 10th Street."

Alphabet City is the part of the East Village which gets its name from Avenues A, B, C and D, which cut across it. It didn't use to be a safe area. In fact, it was a center for drugs and crime. But now things have changed. Today you can find cool cafés, bars and stores in the area.

"So he didn't come from a rich family?" I asked.

"Not at all. Patrick's parents had a hard life. They never lived the American Dream. It wasn't easy for Patrick, either. He's the youngest of six children, so there was no question of the family paying for college. Patrick did it the hard way and paid for everything by working nights at a 24/7 store. He never had the advantages that I had."

"Where do you think he might hide to escape from somebody?" I asked. "Where would he feel safest in this city?"

"I couldn't say for sure. But the area he knows best of all is the East Village," she replied.

"Right. Now, Mrs. O'Neill, I don't want to worry you more than necessary, but I think you're in real danger. The people that broke into your house could come back. I think we should call the NYPD."

Mrs. O'Neill got up from her armchair, walked over to the window and looked out into the street.

At last she spoke: "Mr. Marley, I know you're offering the best advice. But you remember what Patrick said in his message: 'Don't call the NYPD.' Those are his wishes, and I have to follow them."

Chapter 5 *Death by the Hudson River*

It was midday before I got back to East 43rd Street. I picked up a snack at Grand Central Station before returning to the office. It hadn't taken Stella long to find phone numbers for Van Zandts. There were over fifty in all of New York City.

"OK, Stella. We can share this job," I said. "I'll take the first phone book and you can start on the second. Say you're an old friend of O'Neill's and that you're trying to find him."

It was slow and boring work, but I felt it would be worth it in the end. "Good afternoon. Is this Mr. Van Zandt? If I could have a minute of your time? … You see, I'm trying to find an old friend of mine, Patrick O'Neill … Would you know him? … No? OK. Thanks for your time."

As the calls continued, I wasn't feeling too hopeful. Then I got an answering machine. I listened to the message: "I'm sorry I can't get to the phone right now. Leave a message or phone 212-555-01230."

I called the number. The phone was answered after a couple of rings. First the sound of jazz music, then a voice: "Frankie's Cocktail Lounge."

"Good afternoon. Is that Mr. Van Zandt?" I asked.

"Hold on …" I heard the guy shout above the noise, "Frank! Call for you."

Could this finally be the right Van Zandt? I waited patiently.

"Frank Van Zandt speaking."

"If I could have a moment of your time, Mr. Van Zandt," I began. "I've lost the phone number and address of an old friend, Patrick O'Neill. Would you know how I could find him?"

"Oh yeah? I might. Who's asking?" replied Van Zandt.

Not very welcoming, I thought. Time to tell another lie.

"The name's Marley. I'm an old college friend. Patrick and I were at accounting school together."

"If you're so clever, mister, look in the phone book. And don't call again," he added, then put the phone down.

The line went dead – clearly this guy didn't like me asking after O'Neill. This time I felt I was in luck. Perhaps I should visit Frankie's Cocktail Lounge. Before I could organize anything, the phone rang. I picked it up and heard that voice from the past again – Captain Oldenberg.

"Marley!" he shouted. "Your line's been busy for ages. Could I have a minute of your valuable time?"

"Sure. Go ahead." I replied, holding the phone away from my ear.

"Get yourself to the 79th Street Boat Basin. I got something to show you." He laughed.

When Oldenberg laughs, it usually means bad news.

"OK. But why? What's going on?" I asked.

"It's a surprise. But I want you here now," Oldenberg ordered.

I told Stella what was happening. She gave me a smile and said, "Don't get mad at Oldenberg. Remember, we may need his help."

I was back on the subway again, this time to West 79th Street. I walked the two blocks from the subway station west toward the Hudson River, and crossed the Riverside

Park to the boat basin. From here you could see across the river to New Jersey. The temperature had dropped and the sky was full of heavy gray clouds. A cold wind started to blow from the west.

All around the boat basin were houseboats. I've heard it's the cheapest way to live in this city. Ahead I could see NYPD cars in a parking lot near the river. As I got closer, an NYPD cop stopped me and said, "Sorry, sir. You can't enter."

"The name's Marley. Captain Oldenberg's expecting me," I replied.

"OK. Come with me and we'll find the captain," said the cop.

Oldenberg was standing in the parking lot behind a Chevrolet Impala. He was smiling, which always made me feel uncomfortable.

"Take a look at this," said Oldenberg, waving at the car.

Oldenberg moved to the back of the car and opened the trunk. Inside was a dead man.

Oldenberg called to the police doctor. "Could you show me his face again, Doc?" he asked. "OK, Marley, time for your surprise!"

The NYPD doctor was wearing a suit of white material over her clothes, and white plastic gloves and shoes. She carefully took the dead man's head in her hands and moved it round so we could see the face. His skin was gray and his mouth was open. Between his eyes was a hole.

"Marley, meet Ronald Steinmann. Doc, would you tell Mr. Marley what you know?" said Oldenberg.

"I'd say he's been dead about two or three days. A single shot to the head. You see these cuts around his face? This guy was hit hard a number of times before he died. Can't tell you much more just now," the police doctor told me.

Heavy rain began to fall. I was feeling sick. Although I've seen dead bodies before, I still get that same horrible feeling.

"I just checked the license plate. This car belongs to Mr. Patrick O'Neill, Henry Street, Brooklyn. We need to talk, Marley," said Oldenberg. "And I guess you need a drink. Let's go somewhere warmer."

Oldenberg took me to the Boat Basin Café, where he ordered me a double Scotch. The drink was just the right medicine.

"Marley, I got an idea and I think I may be right. Your client could be Patrick O'Neill, an accountant with Ocean Star Finance? Or one of his family?" he asked.

I nodded. The safest thing was to listen and see what Oldenberg wanted.

"Steinmann disappeared some time on Friday afternoon. I've been asking questions at Ocean Star. On Friday morning, people heard Steinmann and O'Neill arguing. This was no conversation between friends. People said it was more like a fight. It was behind closed doors so they couldn't say what they were arguing about. Today Steinmann is found in O'Neill's car, murdered. At the same time nobody seems to know where O'Neill is. You see where this is leading?"

I understood very well. The sick feeling in my stomach started to get stronger.

"I'm talking murder, Marley. I want to question Patrick O'Neill about the murder of Ronald Steinmann. I want to know why O'Neill was paying money into Steinmann's account. Also, the reason why O'Neill had sent him an angry email. It began, 'I didn't think you could be so stupid.' That means I have to find him and I believe you know where he is. You used to be a cop, Marley, so you know the way the police work. If you refuse to tell me, that's a crime."

I held my head in my hands. I could only tell Oldenberg the truth. That wouldn't be what he wanted to hear.

"Believe me, Oldenberg, I'm being completely straight with you. I have no idea where O'Neill is. Yes, my client is his wife. All she knows is that her husband is hiding somewhere."

"OK. Another thing, Marley. I have to question Mrs. O'Neill, but I can't find her. I just get the answering machine every time I call. I need your help," said Oldenberg.

"OK, Oldenberg. I'll see what I can do," I replied.

On the journey back to East 43rd Street, I thought about the information I already knew. I took a fresh page in my notebook and wrote down the facts I knew for sure and the questions that needed answers.

I knew O'Neill had disappeared sometime between Saturday night and Sunday morning. He didn't like his boss, Steinmann, and on Friday he'd argued with him. Also, he had sent an angry email to Steinmann. O'Neill had made large payments to Steinmann and Van Zandt. He was interested in poker. Someone had broken into his house and stolen the hard drive of his computer. Now the police had found Steinmann dead in the trunk of O'Neill's car.

What was I less sure about? What did O'Neill know which put him in danger? Had Steinmann known the same thing? Had O'Neill lost heavily at poker? Was Ocean Star in difficulties? What could explain those payments to Steinmann and Van Zandt? And finally, could a guy like O'Neill kill? The more I thought about it, Ocean Star had to be the key to all the questions.

I called Mrs. O'Neill at her daughter's apartment. "You said that your husband took his car when he disappeared," I said.

"That's right. It's not parked in the street," she replied.

"I'm afraid I have some terrible news. This morning, Steinmann's body was found in the trunk of your husband's car."

I heard a scream over the phone, then nothing.

"Are you still there?" I asked.

"Yes," she replied quietly. "This is just awful. I can't believe it. So what happens now?"

"The police are now looking for your husband," I explained. "I'm sorry, but you'll have to talk to the police."

"I realize I don't have any choice," replied Mrs. O'Neill. "But there's one condition. The meeting should be at your office on East 43rd Street."

Chapter 6 *Questions and answers*

Wednesday, October 6th. Captain Oldenberg and Mrs. O'Neill were in my office at nine o'clock. Mrs. O'Neill was wearing a very fashionable black jacket and skirt with a white blouse. Maybe she did her shopping on Fifth Avenue. Oldenberg was dressed in an ugly brown suit with an orange tie – clothes that had been in fashion sometime during the last century.

Before Oldenberg started questioning Mrs. O'Neill, I told him what I knew about Patrick O'Neill. I was trying to show the captain that O'Neill was just a good ordinary guy, not a murderer.

"As I see it, Patrick O'Neill could be in the middle of something very dangerous," I began. "So far, we have no clear idea of what that might be. We can't be sure if the key to this case is Ocean Star or something that happened between O'Neill and Steinmann – or both.

"Let's move on to O'Neill, the person. We have a happily-married family man who's worked for the same employer for over ten years. In that time he's risen to be second in his department. He's given years of his life to the firm. Also, he has no criminal history."

Oldenberg started to question Mrs. O'Neill. As I thought, his main interest was the argument between O'Neill and Steinmann.

"Mrs. O'Neill," said Oldenberg, "I was told at Ocean Star that your husband and Steinmann argued on Friday before they both disappeared. We don't know what it was about, but people heard Mr. O'Neill shouting. Would you say they worked well together?"

"It was never easy for Patrick," she replied. "Steinmann pushed people hard. Second best was never good enough for him. I can't say Patrick liked him, but he did his work as well as he could."

"Two years ago, your husband had the chance to become the department head. But Lorraine Houston brought in Steinmann. How did your husband feel about this?" asked Oldenberg.

"At the time he was angry, but he learned to accept what had happened. Life has to go on," Mrs. O'Neill replied.

"Could you think of anybody who would want to kill Steinmann?" Oldenberg asked her.

"No," she replied. "OK, so he's not the nicest of guys, but that's no reason for murder."

"Your husband was paying money to Steinmann. Do you have any idea why?" Oldenberg went on.

"None at all," Mrs. O'Neill replied.

Oldenberg continued with questions about the angry email, which Mrs. O'Neill answered patiently. At last, he said, "One more thing, Mrs. O'Neill. Would you agree to a search of your house?"

"I guess I have to," she replied, and handed him her keys. "Go ahead and do it."

"Thanks," he said. "If I'm going to get any further with this case, I must find him. Will you call him?"

Mrs. O'Neill looked him straight in the eyes and said, "That's impossible. Patrick only calls me from pay phones."

"Patrick O'Neill is wanted for murder," Oldenberg said. "And if you, Marley, or you, Mrs. O'Neill, know where he is, and refuse to tell me, that's a crime. You could both find yourselves in jail."

Mrs. O'Neill looked angrily at Oldenberg. If looks could kill, he would be a dead man.

After Oldenberg had left the building, Mrs. O'Neill started to cry.

"I'm sure Patrick has nothing to do with Steinmann's murder," she said. "But what if the police don't believe me? And what if the people who killed Steinmann go after Patrick next?"

"I will find him, I promise you," I said. "But you must be careful. When you get back to Julia's apartment, stay inside, OK? Stella, could you call a cab for Mrs. O'Neill?"

When Mrs. O'Neill had left, I organized some help from an old friend who used to be a policeman like myself. A guy who was as useful as ten NYPD officers – Joe Blaney. He'd taught me more about staying alive on the streets of Manhattan than you could ever learn at Police Academy. He's the sort of person you needed if there was going to be trouble and he knew how to use a gun. I last carried a gun when I was a New York cop. I haven't carried one since and haven't wanted to – but there are times when one is necessary.

I picked up the phone. "Joe, I have work for you. It could be dangerous, so bring a gun. A missing person's in danger, and we're going to find him. Come to East 43rd Street with your car, as soon as you can."

Chapter 7   *Frankie's Cocktail Lounge*

The plan was that Joe and I would pay a visit to Van Zandt and see if he could lead us to O'Neill. Meanwhile, Mrs. O'Neill would come back to the office that afternoon and stay with Stella.

Joe Blaney arrived in his car soon after midday. He's in his middle-sixties, but he's tall and slim with a full head of white hair. Although he's probably twenty years older than me, I'd say he looks younger. Some guys have all the luck.

In the car, Joe pulled his jacket to one side to show me the gun. "Let's hope we don't have to use this, boss," he said. We drove downtown on Second Avenue toward 4th Street. The traffic wasn't too heavy and we soon arrived in the East Village. We went straight along 4th Street to Avenue A. Frankie's Cocktail Lounge was on 5th Street, between Avenues A and B.

Joe stopped the car. Above the double doors, I could read the words: "Frankie's – Cold Drinks, Warm People, Hot Sounds".

"Let's do it," I said.

We went into Frankie's and sat at a table. At first, it seemed almost dark, but soon I could see better. It was a comfortable room with armchairs, sofas, red carpets and the sound of jazz guitar music. We needed clear heads so we ordered two coffees, not the Cocktail Specials. There were no customers at the bar, so I had a look at who was working behind it. A couple of bartenders and someone who I guessed must be the boss. He was medium height with a short black beard, but without a single hair on his head.

"I think we've found Van Zandt," I said, looking toward the bar. "We'll try and have a little talk."

I walked over to the bar with Joe. Van Zandt looked up from some papers he was checking.

"Would you be Mr. Van Zandt?" I asked.

"That's me," he replied. "What can I do for you?"

"Could I talk to you about Patrick O'Neill?" I asked.

"Who are you?" Van Zandt asked carefully and gave me a cold, hard look.

"Nat Marley, licensed private investigator," I said. "I spoke to you on the phone yesterday. I believe you know O'Neill. His wife's very worried about him and I think you could help."

"I don't have to talk to you!" he said angrily.

Suddenly a big strong bartender was standing in front of me.

"You got a problem, boss?" he asked Van Zandt.

"It's OK," I said quietly. "We're not looking for trouble. Look, take my cellphone and press 'Call'. You'll get my office. Ask to talk with O'Neill's wife."

Van Zandt did as I said and spent a couple of minutes checking facts with Mrs. O'Neill. After a while he returned the cellphone and said, "OK. What do you want?" He waved the bartender away and led us to a room behind the bar. Inside, the air didn't smell too fresh – old cigarette smoke. Van Zandt found chairs and sat us at a round table. I introduced Joe, then began questioning Van Zandt.

"I believe that O'Neill has paid you a lot of money?" I asked. "You're not stealing from him, I hope."

35

"It's not robbery," replied Van Zandt. "That's what I won fairly in a poker game. It works both ways. Patrick's an excellent player and I've paid him thousands when I lost. We're old friends. I've known him since we were both kids, working nights at a 24/7 store."

"So explain this," I continued. "Why does a Wall Street accountant come to a back room in the East Village to play poker?"

"I've met several guys like Patrick – hard-working family men who earn good money. But they want a little more from life. Maybe they're just bored so I give them a good time. I know organizing back-room poker games is a crime, but I'm not hurting anybody. These guys have the money – like Patrick's boss, Steinmann. I'm just offering them a service."

"So O'Neill brought Steinmann here?" I asked Van Zandt in surprise.

"Yeah. Once or twice. I don't think Patrick really wanted to, but I guess he couldn't refuse. One night we all lost heavily to Steinmann. He played like poker was his second profession. I had to ask Patrick not to bring him again. It would hurt my bank account too much."

Van Zandt had answered two questions – why O'Neill had made payments to both himself and Steinmann.

"OK. Let's forget the money," I said. "I'm really interested in finding O'Neill. You know he's in some kind of trouble?"

"After reading about Steinmann's murder in the morning papers, I had a good idea what the trouble could be," replied Van Zandt. "Patrick got here soon after midnight, Sunday morning. He said he was in danger, but he wouldn't talk about it. He needed to hide someplace for a few days and was going to check into a hotel around here. He also told me to keep quiet if anyone came asking questions. And one last thing – he told me to expect a letter from his firm. He said it was really important and I should keep it for him."

"If it's arrived, could we take a look?" I asked.

"I guess I could show you," he said.

It was a thick envelope with the address written in O'Neill's handwriting. I took out my pocket knife and cut it open. Inside, I found some papers – probably about twenty pages. At the top of each page I could see the words "Ocean Star Finance" in red and gold letters. On every page, there were lines of numbers.

"You know what this is?" asked Van Zandt.

"I guess some sort of accounts from Ocean Star," I said. "Another guess – this information may have something to do with Steinmann's murder. Mr. Van Zandt, I'd like to thank you for your help. We may be able to reach O'Neill in time. I don't think anyone else knows these papers are here, so could you keep them in a safe place?"

Before Joe and I started searching the East Village, I called Stella to tell her what we'd discovered so far. When I'd finished, Stella said, "Mrs. O'Neill wants to speak with you."

"Mr. Marley, thank you," said Mrs. O'Neill. "You're getting close to Patrick, I can feel it. Please find him and make the police believe that my husband is no killer."

Chapter 8 *The East Village*

Our search area was wide – everything between Fourth Avenue and Avenue D, then everything between East Houston Street and East 14th Street. Within that area are fourteen streets and eight avenues. Now do the math – that makes around eighty blocks. The good news was that if O'Neill was staying in a hotel in the area, like Van Zandt said, we didn't have too many places to check. Most of the hotels are either along Third Avenue or the streets off it.

There were two problems. First, what sort of hotel would O'Neill choose? Somewhere busy, on a crowded street where he wouldn't be noticed? Or would he prefer somewhere quieter and more basic, with less activity? A place where it would be easier to watch and listen. Second, how would we find out if he was staying there? Would he check in under his own name and how could we get the hotel receptionist to tell us if he was there? Hotel receptionists don't give information about their guests to complete strangers.

So we had a plan – I'd say I had a business meeting with O'Neill. To help receptionists believe the story, I'd asked Stella to produce some company information for "Patrick O'Neill Accounting". There was a photo of O'Neill on the front, which I'd hold so the receptionist could see his face.

Time after time at hotels I introduced myself and spoke to the receptionists. "Excuse me, the name's Marley. I have a meeting with Patrick O'Neill. Would you call his room to tell him I'm at reception?"

We had no luck at the more expensive places, which were full of tourists and business people. After asking at a few, we knew what sort of answers to expect: "I'm sorry, sir. Do you have the correct hotel? ... I wish I could help you, but ..."

Hour after hour, our search area grew wider. We had moved away from Third Avenue, deeper into the center of the East Village, toward Alphabet City.

At some of the cheaper places, the receptionists were less patient: "We got nobody by that name staying here, mister ... Look, mister, I just work here. It's not my job to remember faces."

We continued until early evening. It was six thirty, not long before sunset, and the sky in the west was growing pink. We just had one or two more places to check in Alphabet City. The next hotel, the Madigan Inn on Avenue B, looked like an ugly, dirty place, but the receptionist was helpful.

I asked the usual questions and made sure that she could see O'Neill's photo. Then the surprise – I could see from the look on her face that she knew something. "Sure I know the guy," she said. "But not by the name of O'Neill. I don't know if I'm allowed to say ..."

I showed her my investigator's license and said, "The truth is, this guy's life is in danger. I'm working for his family and we need to find him quickly, before someone else does."

She believed me and turned to check the computer. "Yeah, there he is," she said. "He stayed for one night and checked out yesterday. The name he gave was Brendan Touhey."

"Can you tell me anything more?" I asked. "Did he have any visitors? How did he spend his time?"

"Well, he asked for a room on the street. That seemed to be important. He didn't have any visitors and spent most of the time in his room. I think he was watching the street. Or that's what I thought when I looked up at his window."

"Thanks," I said. "You've been really helpful."

"You could ask at our other hotel," she said. "I could phone ahead to tell them to expect you. It's the Metro, on Avenue C between 4th and 3rd."

"Please. If you would," I replied.

As we left, I said to Joe, "At last we're getting somewhere. I think I know what he's doing. Just staying a night at one place, then moving on."

Joe suddenly stopped in front of the door to the street. "Nat, you see that car just across the street?"

"The black one?" I asked.

"That's it. I think I've seen it before. Outside your office, but I couldn't be too sure," Joe went on.

I studied the car carefully. A Lexus, which costs serious money. Three guys with dark glasses were inside. It was starting to get dark and I've never liked guys who wear sunglasses at night. I had a horrible feeling that those people meant trouble.

Then the driver looked toward us and the car quickly moved along the avenue. In the poor light, I couldn't read the license plate.

"What do you think, boss?" asked Joe. "Are they following us?"

The streetlights had now come on. Under their yellow light I could see the answer to Joe's question. On the road beside Joe's car was a knife. There was no air in two of the tires so it was impossible to drive.

Now I realized what was happening. Those guys had followed us, hoping we would lead them to O'Neill. They knew we were checking hotels, and the Metro was the last one in the area. They wanted to make sure they got there first.

We ran across to Avenue C, but we were losing valuable time. The Metro, like the last hotel, looked as if nobody cared for it. The receptionist, though, was friendly and welcomed us with a smile.

"Hi, I'm Gina," she said. "You guys didn't need to hurry. We got—"

I stopped her and said, "The receptionist at the Madigan just phoned ahead and told you to expect us. We're looking for Patrick O'Neill. He's in danger and might be using a different name. Has anyone asked for him?" I showed her O'Neill's photograph.

"Oh yes," said Gina. "He's staying here, but under the name of Bernard Delaney. Nice, quiet guy. He stays in his room most of the time. There's something I don't understand. You're the second group of people asking about him. The others went up to his room five minutes ago, but they just left."

"What others?" I shouted.

"Three guys in black suits and dark glasses," she replied. "I thought they were the ones I was expecting."

"Did O'Neill leave with them?" I asked.

"No," Gina replied.

"Oh my God! Give me the room number quick!" I shouted. "I hope we're not too late!"

Chapter 9 *The Metro, Avenue C*

"Second floor, Room 219," said Gina.

No time to lose. Joe and I ran upstairs to the room. The door was open and the lock was broken. Inside, we could see that someone had quickly searched the room. An empty travel bag was lying on the floor. The blankets had been pulled off the bed, and clothes thrown around the room.

"O'Neill's not here, but those other guys won't be far away," I said. "I don't like this one bit. Let's get back to the lobby."

At the desk, I made a 911 call for the police, described the three guys and their car, and said, "I believe they're looking for Patrick O'Neill, who's staying at this hotel."

We walked out onto the street to wait for the police, who I knew ought to be here in minutes. But things now happened very quickly. A guy in dark glasses was standing opposite us, across the road. He laughed and said, "I guess you ain't going no place fast."

Then he began to cross the street, like he didn't need to hurry. He spoke again: "You guys. Just tell me where O'Neill is. Then you can go home and forget you ever saw me."

He wanted O'Neill, but we had no idea where he might be. I looked left and right along the street. On either side of us was a guy in a black suit walking slowly toward us. Both of them were carrying guns. We had no place to run, no place to hide.

Luckily, Joe was thinking more quickly than me. "Back inside the hotel, now!" he shouted and pushed me toward the entrance.

We turned and ran inside. Behind us I could hear the sound of running feet as they chased after us. "On the floor, behind the desk, now!" said Joe.

There was no time to say "If you please, ma'am" as I threw Gina to the ground. The front door opened with a crash, but Joe was ready for them. I heard two shots, followed by a scream, then everything was quiet. There was a cloud of smoke from the shots in the air. Joe was now at the desk.

"I think I hit one, but they'll be back," said Joe. "We have to hurry. Gina, you got to help us! Is there a back entrance?"

"Through here," replied Gina. "Follow me."

She led us through a door behind the desk, then down some steps. Behind us I heard a crash as the men in black returned. We were now hurrying through the hotel kitchen. I heard shouts and feet on the stairs. They were getting close.

"Turn off any lights and lock doors behind us if you can," I told Gina.

I decided to make things more difficult for the guys following us. I pulled glasses and bottles to the floor. We reached the back door just as we heard the men coming into the kitchen. There was a shot, which left a hole in the wall beside me. That was much too close. A second later, the room was in complete darkness as Gina turned off the lights. There were shouts as one of the guys fell over.

"Up these steps. Hurry!" said Gina.

We were now outside in the cold night air. We went up a few more steps, then out into a narrow street behind the hotel. In the darkness, I could just see back entrances to buildings along Avenue C. We had passed a few doors when Gina suddenly stopped. "I don't know what to do!" she screamed.

"Through this door, quickly," I ordered. "And get down!"

We hit the ground behind some boxes. It didn't smell too clean down there, but this wasn't the time to worry about the dry cleaner's bill. Gina had started to cry, so I put my hand over her mouth to keep her quiet.

"Don't make a sound,' Joe whispered. "With luck, the NYPD should arrive before they find us."

As we hid there in the darkness, we heard feet running to the left and right along the narrow street. Then we heard the steps returning more slowly, and voices.

"They got to be here someplace," said one. "They can't have gotten far."

"Start with these doors," said another. "Let's see where they're hiding."

There was crash after crash as the doors were opened. More shots. Well, that's one way to unlock a door if you don't have the key. The noise was now getting closer. I kept my hand over Gina's mouth. Her body was shaking. Finally, above the crashes and shots, a new but very welcome sound. The scream of a police car.

"It's the cops. Let's get out of here!" shouted a voice on the other side of the door.

We heard them running back toward the hotel. Then all went quiet. After waiting a few minutes, I decided it was safe to come out.

Back inside the hotel kitchen, it looked like the morning after a wild party. We walked carefully around the broken glasses and bottles on the floor. In the hotel lobby, two guys in black suits were lying on the floor. Above them stood two NYPD cops.

"Am I pleased to see you!" I said. "I'm Nat Marley, licensed private investigator. Did you catch all three of them?"

"Yes, sir. The other one is outside with the sergeant. He'll need an ambulance," said one of the cops.

"We got here just in time," said the other. "Captain Oldenberg's on his way. He'll need to question you."

Gina was feeling better. Her suit was black with dirt and oil. Mine didn't look much cleaner, though. Now I started to shake. It's always the same. It never hits me at the time, but later, when I realize I'm lucky to be alive.

"I guess I could make everyone coffee," said Gina.

"That'd be great." But then I had a sudden thought and shouted, "Joe, upstairs now!"

We ran back up to Room 219. The door was closed and when I knocked there was no reply. I put my ear to the door and listened. Somebody was moving around in the room. I tried to open the door, but there was something against it on the other side. However, it wasn't strong enough for Joe's boot and flew open. Inside we saw a man holding the travel bag.

He threw the bag into Joe's face and tried to push past me. But I was able to catch his coat and pull him to the floor. I looked at him closely – a middle-aged guy with gray hair and black metal glasses – Patrick O'Neill.

"Don't be afraid!" I said. "I'm Nat Marley, private investigator. I'm working for your wife, Joyce. You're going be safe. It's time to stop running."

Chapter 10 *Time to fight back*

There was a hopeless look in O'Neill's eyes. His lips moved, but he couldn't speak. I shook his shoulders and made him look straight at me. "Listen, we're the good guys. You're out of danger. Your wife sent us to find you."

He still seemed to be unsure, so I pulled him to his feet and tried again. "Here's my cellphone. It's calling my office number. As soon as my personal assistant answers, ask to speak to Joyce."

We waited while he spoke to his wife. He sat down on the bed as he talked. Now he looked tired and weak, like a lost child.

"If you don't mind, Mr. O'Neill, I need to talk to my personal assistant now," I said. He returned my cellphone.

"Stella, listen carefully," I said. "Call a cab, and take Mrs. O'Neill to Frankie's Cocktail Lounge on 5th Street. We're going to meet you there as soon as possible. We need to make Oldenberg believe that O'Neill is not Steinmann's killer."

Now O'Neill was beginning to look more normal. "I guess I should say sorry," he said. "How did you know where to find me?"

"I can explain that," I replied. "Through information in your bank accounts, we learned that you'd made payments to a Van Zandt. That's how we found your old friend Frank."

"So you know about the poker games," said O'Neill. "When I told Joyce I was working late, I was actually—"

"It doesn't matter now," I said. "Van Zandt told us that you'd checked into a hotel somewhere in the East Village. You heard about Steinmann's murder? The police think you did it, but I didn't think that could be true. So I thought you might be in danger too. But how did you get away from the guys in black suits?"

"I was watching the street from my window," began O'Neill. "I saw them arrive and thought they had to be bad news. I ran up to the top floor and hid in a blanket cupboard. I'd been up there for about ten minutes when I heard the shots. So I stayed there until I heard the police car arrive and came down to my floor. When I looked out of my window again, I could see the sergeant outside with one of them. Finally, I thought it was safe enough to escape."

"That letter you sent to Van Zandt. What do all those numbers mean?" I asked.

"They're the reason why Steinmann was murdered," replied O'Neill.

Suddenly, there was someone at the door. It was Captain Oldenberg. He looked around, shook his head and asked in a tired voice, "Would you mind telling me what's going on, Marley?"

"Oldenberg, let me introduce Mr. Patrick O'Neill. Mr. O'Neill was almost murdered here tonight. Thanks to the sergeant and his team, we're all still alive. Mr. O'Neill has a story to tell you. I believe that once you know all the facts, it will be clear that he can't be Steinmann's killer."

"I'm listening, Marley," said Oldenberg. "But whether he's the killer is for the police to decide, not you."

"Mr. O'Neill can show you all the information you need," I continued. "If you agree, it means a quick journey to Frankie's Cocktail Lounge on 5th Street. Everything's there."

"Agreed," said Oldenberg. "But for the moment, O'Neill, you're still wanted for murder, and that means you're my prisoner. Anyway, I guess Police Headquarters will be rather safer than this hotel."

We all went downstairs, back to reception, where Oldenberg organized everyone. "Sergeant, you're coming with me and O'Neill. Have your men take away the other two prisoners and one officer should stay with the guy who was shot."

Joe had to leave and get some help with his car. Oldenberg drove us through the East Village back to 5th Street. Frankie's Cocktail Lounge was now noisy with the evening crowd. A jazz band was getting ready to play. I saw Stella and Mrs. O'Neill sitting at a corner table, waiting for us to arrive.

"Your husband's outside, Mrs. O'Neill," I told her. "If you could be patient for a few more minutes, I'll find somewhere less public to talk."

I went over to the bar and shouted above the noise to the bartender. "I need to speak to Frank. Where can I find him?"

"In the back room," answered the bartender. "Just go straight through."

I coughed as I entered because the air was heavy with cigarette smoke. "O'Neill's outside with the police," I said. "Could we meet in here? Oh, and we'll need that envelope."

"Sure. Let's get some fresh air in here," said Van Zandt as he threw open a window. Oldenberg brought O'Neill into the room, and Stella followed with Mrs. O'Neill.

As soon as everybody was inside the office, O'Neill took his wife in his arms. "It's wonderful to see you again, Joyce," he said. "I'm going to stop hiding. Now it's time to fight back."

"Patrick, I've been so worried for you," she said. "What's been happening? Why all these secrets?"

"There's so much to explain," replied O'Neill. "I'll tell you everything, I promise. But first, I have to make the captain understand that I'm not to blame for Steinmann's death."

O'Neill turned to Oldenberg and opened the envelope. He took out the papers and laid them on the table. He said, "These are secret papers from the Ocean Star president's office. There's enough information here to send Lorraine Houston to jail."

"If you could keep it short," said Oldenberg.

"OK. Ocean Star is an investment firm. Its business is making money for its clients," continued O'Neill. "How do they do this? By investing clients' money in the international money markets – or that's what should happen. Look at this page. It's organized in two halves, so let's compare the two sides. On the left the numbers show money that was paid to clients – often a fifteen per cent return. On the right we see what the firm actually made from investments. Surprise, surprise! These numbers are far less. You realize what this means?"

"Go on, tell me," said Oldenberg. "You're the accountant."

"Ocean Star can't possibly earn enough from its investments to pay big money to the clients and millions to the president. It's using the money from new clients to pay the old clients. As long as it continues to get large numbers of new clients, this can work, and people think it's the smartest firm on Wall Street. However, it's a serious crime. I believe that's why Steinmann was murdered. He knew about it too after I showed him these accounts, and he talked to Houston. I want to make all this public, and now I don't care if it destroys Ocean Star at the same time. Is that clear, Captain?"

"More or less," replied Oldenberg. "If I could take those papers … Thanks. But there are a lot more questions which I want answered. We'll continue at Police Headquarters. Mr. O'Neill, you're still my prisoner."

Chapter 11 *O'Neill's story*

At Police Headquarters, Oldenberg led us up to his office. I'd sent Stella home – at least one of us should try and get a good night's sleep. Mrs. O'Neill wouldn't leave her husband.

Inside Oldenberg's office, it couldn't be more different from the offices I'd seen at Ocean Star. The walls were a dirty green color and there was no carpeting on the floor. "Basic" was the best word to describe it. Oldenberg had ordered coffee and sandwiches for everybody. At least the NYPD coffee tasted better than it used to when I was a cop.

"You have a story to tell us, Mr. O'Neill," said Oldenberg. "I want to know everything about you, Steinmann and Ocean Star."

"OK. Two years ago, the old department head moved to another firm," began O'Neill. "I'd worked at Ocean Star for over eight years and I thought I had a good chance of getting the job. I was wrong – the president, Lorraine Houston, had decided to bring in someone new. Someone who didn't care who he hurt.

"So I went on with my work and did what was necessary. With Steinmann as head of department, the firm was making even more money than before. Houston thought he was wonderful, but people who were working with me thought the opposite. Steinmann loved to push people hard.

"A year ago, I asked Steinmann how the firm could continue paying so much money to its clients. The money our department made from clients' investments wasn't that high. I did the math again and still didn't understand. Where was the money coming from? I was worried, but Steinmann promised me that there were no problems. He said, 'Just do your job and don't ask too many questions. She knows what she's doing on the top floor.'

"The 'top floor' is where Lorraine Houston has her offices. Steinmann hoped to get his own office there some day. It seemed impossible to talk to him, so I kept my mouth shut. Time passed and Ocean Star went on paying out big money to its clients. Then, on Friday morning last week, I received the information that could destroy the firm and send Lorraine Houston to jail.

"It happened by chance. I got a letter from Houston's office. At first I didn't understand why I'd been sent a hard copy of the accounts – usually everything like that is sent through office email. I soon realized that it had been a mistake. Houston's personal assistant had sent me an envelope which was meant to go to the vice-president.

"I knew I shouldn't, but I continued reading. As I read, I was more and more surprised. Now I understood that the public accounts weren't the truth. These were secret accounts, which weren't on computer. They showed that Ocean Star was using the money from its new clients to pay the old ones. Now I understood how Houston had so much to spend on her cars, homes, clothes and vacations.

"I didn't like the idea, but I thought I should talk with Steinmann. I knew I had to be careful, so I made a copy of the accounts to show him. What about the ones I'd received? How could I get the information out of the building safely? I had an idea – I put the accounts in an envelope and addressed it to my old friend Frank Van Zandt. Then I left the building for five minutes and dropped the envelope in the nearest mailbox.

"Later that morning, I spoke with Steinmann, and gave him the copy of the accounts. He was immediately very interested. He laughed and said, 'So that's how she does it. You've done the right thing. I'll go straight upstairs and talk with Houston. With this information, I could make a lot of money. Maybe I'll share some with you.'

"His plan was to ask Houston to pay him to keep quiet. I became really angry with him and tried to make him change his mind. But he refused. He wouldn't listen to me and went up to the top floor. Now I knew that I could be in real trouble because Steinmann had gotten the accounts from me. I wasn't sure what to do, but my first move was to get out of the office quick.

"I told my personal assistant that I'd had an awful headache all day and had to go home. Back home, I waited a couple of hours, then made some phone calls. First I called Steinmann's personal assistant. She told me that Steinmann's desk was empty and his computer was gone, but she couldn't tell me anything more. I sent Steinmann an angry email to his home computer. I wrote something like, 'I didn't think you could be so stupid. I can't believe what you've done.'

"The next day, I felt bad about what I'd said in the email, so I tried to phone Steinmann. His wife answered and told me that he hadn't come home, and she was very worried. That night, I stayed up late thinking about what I should do. Just before midnight I got a call. Someone said, 'You have information which belongs to the firm. Return this information to Ms. Houston by midday tomorrow if you want to stay alive.'

"How could I return the accounts? They were in the U.S. Mail. So I thought the safest thing to do was to hide. I wrote a note for Joyce and left in the middle of the night. Looking back, maybe it wasn't the most intelligent decision. I packed a bag, left by the back entrance, took a cab to Frank Van Zandt's place. I can promise you I left my car on Henry Street. I told Frank to expect the letter with the accounts, then I checked into a hotel. On Monday morning I took out $10,000 from the bank so I wouldn't need to use any credit cards. I think you know the rest of the story."

"Thanks, Mr. O'Neill," said Oldenberg. "That's very helpful."

Oldenberg led me to another office. He thought for a few moments, then said, "Marley, I need some advice. My problem is this – if I accept that Houston ordered Steinmann's murder, how can I show that it's true?"

"If you'll allow me, Captain," I said. "I got an idea that just might work."

Chapter 12 *If the price is right*

What if nobody knew that O'Neill was at Police Headquarters? That would give us the chance to tell some clever lies – lies that might give us the advantage. I shared my ideas with the captain.

"We don't know for sure, but let's say Lorraine Houston planned Steinmann's murder," I began. "She's killed one person and she wants O'Neill badly enough to kill again. Why don't we try out this plan? Give the news of what happened at the Metro Hotel tonight to the newspapers, TV and radio stations. Some of it can be true, but a few things can be changed. We tell them that O'Neill escaped and is believed to be somewhere in the East Village area. Houston will be very afraid. She has a lot to lose if she doesn't find O'Neill first and stop him from talking."

"OK, Marley. So far, so good. What next?" asked Oldenberg.

"If you agree, I could speak with her. I'll tell her I have something to sell – the secret accounts."

"Go on," said Oldenberg. "I'm interested. But why you? Why couldn't an NYPD officer do it?"

"I'll tell her I've found O'Neill and am keeping him someplace safe – where she'll never find him. I'll also tell her I have the accounts, which I'll offer to sell if the price is right. I'll make her an offer which she can't refuse. For $100,000 I'll return the accounts to her and give O'Neill to the police. Houston will think she has won. The secret accounts will be safe and O'Neill will be in jail for Steinmann's murder. I'll meet with her, then try and get her to talk."

"Come on, Marley. Get real!" said Oldenberg. "You think a hard businesswoman like Houston is just going to say, 'Oh, by the way, I ordered Steinmann's murder.'"

"I'll let her think I'm the same sort of person as her," I continued. "A businessman who doesn't care how he earns his money or who he hurts. If she feels comfortable with me, then we might get the truth."

"This had better work, Marley. I hope you're a good enough actor," said Oldenberg.

"Believe me, Oldenberg, on a good day I could win Oscars," I told him.

"All right. We'll do it," replied Oldenberg. "This could be dangerous. You know that as well as I do. You'll need a full NYPD team behind you. I'll organize that as soon as you and Houston have a time and a place to meet. So now I'll talk to the newspapers and Houston will think that O'Neill is still in hiding."

"OK. And one more thing," I said. "Mrs. O'Neill and her daughter Julia could be in real danger. Could you move them to an NYPD safe house?"

"Consider it done," said Oldenberg.

* * *

Wednesday had been a very long day. I got home at three o'clock in the morning and I was so tired that I felt like a dead man walking. I fell into bed and slept well.

The next morning I woke up late, feeling much better. After quickly getting dressed, I ran down to the nearest newsstand and picked up the morning newspapers. I took the papers into Slim Pete's Diner on Main Street to read more carefully. The name "Slim" is a joke. Actually, he has a serious weight problem.

"What'll it be, Mr. Marley?" asked Pete with a big smile.

"Eggs, pancakes and bacon," I answered. "And make that coffee strong, will you?"

"You got it. So what's the famous Mr. Marley doing today?" asked Pete. "Helping New York's Finest win the war against crime?"

"Something like that," I replied.

"New York's Finest" – that's what people call the NYPD. I never thought of myself as one of the "Finest" when I was a cop and I never thought I was fighting a war. I was just doing my job. If there was a little less crime on the streets by the end of the day, that was good enough for me.

I read through the newspapers. Oldenberg had done an excellent job. The O'Neill story was on all the front pages. The headline of the *Daily News* read, "NYPD's MOST WANTED ESCAPES". The *New York Post* headline made me smile: "KILLER ACCOUNTANT ON THE RUN". There was some truth, but the rest of the story sounded like something from the movies: "This man is both intelligent and dangerous," said Captain Oldenberg. This wasn't the O'Neill that I knew.

While I ate my breakfast, I watched the TV news. Their reporter said, "This is Cindy Lu outside the Metro Hotel on Avenue C. Here, last night, NYPD officers almost caught Patrick O'Neill, the man wanted for the murder of Ronald Steinmann …"

"Well done, Oldenberg," I thought. Now Houston would get a clear message. Neither her people nor the NYPD had found O'Neill, so she still had a real problem on her hands. I hoped she was one very worried woman.

I got to the office by ten o'clock. Stella had already been there a couple of hours. "That was quite a day, yesterday. You feeling OK, now?" she asked.

"A lot better," I replied. "And thank you for taking care of Mrs. O'Neill all day. With luck, we're going to send Lorraine Houston to jail."

During the morning I agreed on a plan with Oldenberg. I would meet with Houston in a public area, the kind of place where it would be easy for an NYPD team to watch and wait. Our choice was Battery Park, at the foot of Manhattan, with its tall trees and green grass. This is where New York meets the ocean. From here you can look across Upper New York Bay to the Statue of Liberty and Staten Island.

I tried to get through to Houston on my cellphone, but her personal assistant wouldn't allow me to speak with her. "I'm sorry, sir, but Ms. Houston isn't taking any calls," she said.

I wasn't going to take "no" for an answer. "Listen carefully and just do what I say. Your boss lost something of great importance. Tell her I've found it and want to return it to her. I'll call back in ten minutes and expect to speak with her in person. Understood?"

"Careful, now," I told myself. "No mistakes." I waited a full fifteen minutes before calling back. People think less clearly when they get impatient. This time I got ahold of Houston immediately.

"Who are you and what do you want?" she asked crossly.

"The name's Marley. I was working for Mr. O'Neill. He found some interesting papers of yours, which he gave me to look after. Now I'm working for myself and I thought that you might like to have those papers back. I'll make this offer even more generous. The police will be very interested when I tell them where O'Neill is. The price is $100,000. Wait in your office for my call at eight o'clock tomorrow morning."

"What?" began Houston.

"That's it, lady!" I shouted. "Be ready in your office, eight o'clock tomorrow with $100,000, OK? And don't think of doing anything clever or every newspaper in this city will know the truth about Ocean Star's accounts."

With that, I ended the call. I felt very pleased with myself. Would I still feel so pleased tomorrow?

Chapter 13   *Battery Park*

Friday, October 8th, 7:00 a.m. I was on my way from Grand Central Station to Bowling Green on a number five train. This subway station is just north of Battery Park, which was where I was going to meet Lorraine Houston.

Battery Park is a public area where it would be easier for the NYPD team to watch and wait. I thought that Houston would feel uncomfortable away from the deep carpets and expensive furniture of her offices.

From the subway station, it was just a few minutes' walk to Battery Park. I walked across to the Sphere, a famous piece of public art at the north end of the park – a large gold metal ball, as tall as a house. Oldenberg's team was already waiting there with hidden cameras, though you wouldn't know they were police officers. Two young guys talking on a seat. A couple standing under an umbrella. Their orders were to watch and wait. But if I waved my hat, they would immediately help me.

The sky was full of black clouds and it was starting to rain. I put up my umbrella and looked at my watch. It was eight o'clock, time to call Houston.

"Ms. Houston? I'm waiting for you," I said. "Bring the money and come alone. If there's any trouble, my personal assistant has a copy of your accounts ready to email to every newspaper in New York. If all goes to plan, she'll destroy that copy."

"OK. That's understood," she replied. "How do I know you're telling the truth?"

"Ask yourself this question: What will happen if you don't believe me? I'll need your cellphone number … Thanks. Now, leave the building and wait outside the front entrance."

I let her wait a few minutes in the cold. I wanted her to feel angry and impatient by the time she arrived at Battery Park. Now for my next call.

"So sorry to keep you waiting," I lied. "You see a tall white-haired guy in a dark green overcoat, carrying a copy of the *Wall Street Journal*? He should be opposite you, standing by a cab." Houston said she could see him.

"That's my assistant, Mr. Blaney. Go and talk with him," I continued. "He has a cab waiting for you."

We had to make sure that Houston arrived alone. Joe Blaney's job was to make sure that she took our cab – a cab with an NYPD driver. Houston was going to be taken on a little tour of Lower Manhattan. We were going to take our time and make sure she was in a very bad mood by the time she met me.

Thirty minutes later I called Houston again.

"Tell the driver to drop you at the north entrance to Battery Park, opposite Bowling Green. Then walk south to the Sphere. You'll see me holding a blue and white golf umbrella. By the way, you don't need to pay the driver. Hope you enjoyed your sightseeing."

I wouldn't like to repeat Houston's reply – such bad language! The rain was beginning to fall more heavily as I saw her. She was tall and slim and was wearing a red suit with a short skirt that showed a lot of leg. She really wasn't dressed for the weather. I turned on my little secret recorder. I waved to her and sat on a park seat under the trees opposite the Sphere.

"This had better be good, Marley," she said. "Do you have my papers?"

"Not so fast," I replied. "Do you have my money?"

She put her case on her knees and opened it. Inside, it was packed with hundred-dollar bills.

"Count it if you like," she said.

"Don't you think the park looks lovely in fall?" I asked.

"I don't have all day. Hurry up and give me the papers," she said impatiently.

I slowly reached into my case and took out an envelope, which I gave to her. Then I reached into my coat pocket for my cellphone.

Houston took a single piece of paper out of the envelope and looked at me like a dog which was about to bite.

"Give me the rest of the accounts, Marley, or you're dead meat!" She had taken a small gun out of her purse and was pressing it into my side.

"Not very intelligent, Ms. Houston," I said. "Remember, if anything happens to me, my personal assistant will email your accounts to every newspaper in this city. If I press 'Send', my personal assistant gets that message. Also, shooting people in public isn't a good idea. You'll get the rest of the papers. Just be patient. Like any good businessman, I like to count my money first."

She gave me a cold, hard look through narrow eyes, then put the gun back in her purse. Now she was beginning to shake with the cold.

"Here, take my overcoat," I said.

She took the coat and put it over her shoulders. She smiled for the first time and thanked me. Now I felt I might have the advantage.

I quickly checked the money, then took a second envelope from my case and held it in front of her.

"There must be some very important information here. You're one smart businesswoman, Ms. Houston, and a good employer. I like the way you find answers to problems with your people. Like sending Steinmann on his final drive in O'Neill's car. Good work. The police think that O'Neill is the killer. That way you can be completely sure it's the end of your trouble with those two. As soon as I tell the police where O'Neill is, you're safe."

She smiled again. "You're a smart guy. I'm sorry about Steinmann. He was good at his job, until he started to think he was smarter than me. I couldn't let him tell me what to do. I had to get rid of him."

At last I had it, and everything was on the recorder. I passed her the second envelope. She opened it quickly, took out the papers and counted them.

"Looks like it's all here. It's been good doing business with you," she said, and returned my overcoat. "Now just make sure the police get ahold of O'Neill."

As she walked away, I called to her, "Actually, Ms. Houston, I got a message from O'Neill. He'd like to tell you, 'Smile! You're on a police camera!'"

I waved my hat in the air. Houston screamed and pulled out her gun, but in seconds the NYPD team was all around her. She dropped the gun and fell to the ground.

A minute ago she had been the president of Ocean Star Finance and a very rich woman. Now she was going to spend many years in jail.

I called Oldenberg to tell him the news. "Good work, Marley!" he said. "O'Neill will soon be a free man."

The rain had stopped and the sun had begun to break through the heavy clouds. In the sunshine, leaves were dropping from the trees and turning in the wind. The air from the ocean smelled fresh and clean. It felt good to be alive. I should spend more time in this city's parks.